Slant Light

Slant Light

Sarah Westcott

First published 2016 by
Liverpool University Press
4 Cambridge Street
Liverpool
L69 7ZU

British Library Cataloguing-in-Publication data
A British Library CIP record is available

ISBN 978-1-78138-292-9 softback

Typeset by Carnegie Book Production, Lancaster
Printed and bound in Poland by BooksFactory.co.uk

For Patrick, Bridget and Gabriel

Contents

Bats

Let us begin at slant light
with cut felt flickers,
unhooding cubic skulls,
furtive and hungry.

Trace our loopy symmetries
beneath the canopy as we feed,
follow our dance with open faces –
long diverged from the birds.

You cannot hear us but you'll feel
our hunting song across your teeth
defiling the laws of physics
with frequencies beyond this.

Watch our velvet forms take on
three dimensions or four
as we vanish into sky space,
a filigree of apple tree

bursting into fret-work,
scraps of jinking balsa,
flicking the Vs, skimming
odd quick trajectories.

We are fickle as kits,
wombed and jewelled
with kidneys, ovaries,
rows of studded teats.

Born to kill, we are strung
on struts of steel; dissolve
in darkness to anti-matter,
turning widdershins,

bewilderingly separate,
a tapestry of gremlin flight
angling on planes of sound,
almost sightless, blind-to-green.

Turn your ears towards us,
bearing truths in our pitch and fall;
forest-worlds and gardens returned
in sonic negative, transformed.

Hold us in dry hands
when you find us in the woods,
stroke our underbellies
with something approaching tenderness.

Inklings

Sometimes when we make love near the window
I can almost feel them waiting in the corners,
whispering in dusty spaces above the wardrobe,
their breath in drifts of light across the glaucous room,
and sometimes I glimpse filaments brushing against the panes,
delicate as spider silk – sense shifts in matter, stirrings,
and then it doesn't take much to bring them into our warm bed,
to call them down, the two of us moving together,
moulding them out of our hearts like clay,
with the mortar and pestle of our bodies,
the cups and planes of our hips
and thighbones working like engines all greased with blood and longing,
for soon we are reaching towards shining crowns,
our fingers straining to touch them,
and breathing out in one long rush into their starry lungs,
and sometimes afterwards if we are still they might come into focus,
step forward into the light, already entirely themselves.

Spring Wood

tap
      tap
knocking softly, let me in

leaves unlearning the cold,
         old cold loosening as moult

dress rags falling

warmth, faint,
seeps into layers of song,
nets flung and falling

the rain – a wealth of it
a thousand tiny feet, or
beats,

points of impact opening
seeds, seed-heads,
germ notes

      deliberate I draw
sleeves of light over beech,
old burrs young,

      – ears prink,
sun just warm enough to wake a hog –

hear my wagtail,
bending and dipping, sweet fulcrum –

all my minnow fry
crows, larking,
high mud banks I'll lick

all of me cloaked in green
spreads across the earth

beetles mealing away
mycelium threading
moles marrowing my veins

river stirs and beds her curves to mine
catching light and young leaves,

damp violet,
                quiet ash keys

Form

Not snail, exactly –
epithelial with a tensile foot

like a surfboard with nerves,
responsive as any insect

but wet, wet as reed beds,
sunk root feeding deeply in the dark.

Not mussel, either, nor quilled
but mother, a good mother

of pearl, pressed with an energy
that sets her edges to fact

each radial spoke
angled in relative truth

each fold into a further chamber
enfolding something of itself.

Here, beneath my finger like braille,
the clearest patterns

turning and returning
in my palm.

Downy Mildew

'People thought fungi repulsive, and I wanted
to show how beautiful they can be.'

Dillon Weston

Here, in the looking –
beyond the rot,
a duplicity.

*

The glass is molasses;
I tease it with pliers
into a raft of mycelium,

fruiting and threading,
an asexual labour
of love,

hyaline, gutless,
brittle beauty tinted pink
hardening under the light.

And how to make the roots?
    Not quite on little cat feet,
        not quite a tub with lion's claws,

a bit like a faun, sprung
    on tendon and bone
        or something reptilian on hot sand

caught in the act of movement
    exact as notes, the placement
      and the lift –

From this matter
I draw five hyphae-with-intent
to spread into fruiting bodies

beaded sporocarps,
where sweetness pools and drips
and yet to touch, the finest hairs

melt to nothing
on my skin, too delicate
for cellulose or lignin.

*

Contingent as mist
we rise up like little loaves
with dark spores

blaze our hackles, haring
across the greenest crucifers,
sinking into pulp,

waiting for the softest
fruits to fall.

*

Here, in the looking –
beyond the rot, we float,
wait for you to see.

Milia

We hear the first notes as we cry,
the insistence of air
shocking us all, timpani vibrating
as we sense the bright world.

We don't know why we are here
no more nor less than what we are
and were before –
                              wingless, hairy

we root for the dark stalk, its dripping music
follow the milk song,
the echo of our mothers' voices,
each mouthful a stay against the loss –

our skins raise mild white pustules in the light –
for the dark is never as dark again
and as we sleep our eyes roll back
to gaze at where we come from.

For the Love of Young Leaf

You silent ripple of wet hem over slate,
rubber necked in the greening growth –
globular lunar snouter of dark ways,
your bovine, blunted downward gaze beyond
opened sky to micro-scraps of food.

The brittle ear you slide along the ground,
your humped rebuke to beaks, bones and sun,
your stalky peer, erectile eyes, old mouth
your craquelure on granite, your garland
of quiet effort looped around our feet.

Your space-ship purity of vision,
your glowing point of will scooping a trench,
the string of pearls you drop into the earth
softly as butter out of your soft foot,
opaque as babies' fingernails, but tough.

The infinite proportions of your form,
solidified before we learned to count,
the appetite we share that draws us on,
to fall upon the earth, then rise again,
to follow you with slow and greedy passion.

Flowers

The language of flowers grows further
than pores and bracts and petioles
fine leaflets, visible cells
pilose dog rose opening.

The ray floret catches awareness,
funnels sticky stigma,
down to the spur, the fused keel,
through the speculum.

Caught in the panicle, our eyes
are dark, sweet pomes,
words ripen like samara –
winged seeds which gyrate as they fall.

Lily

I'm open,
flower face up to the light,
stamens, hyphae threading
deep into me, and you bend
as if tending, ardently, to well-
turned soil, thumbing and tasting,
planting deep gold,
seeds that will root and bloom
into white lillies round other beds,
all of us down on our knees with the smell.

The Mariposa Trees

Fallen Monarch

Still, I speak of the battle,
how wind lifted seeds from my arms,
and my kingdom fell to the saplings.

I rot in my resting place,
hide pocked with arrow slots and snow.
You thought me stunned, I bleed

floral channels, rivulets of lichen,
flanks drinking sun,
not over the act of being alive,

yet Gullivered, unable to move
til earth heaves me to my river bed
and I can float, weightless as a seed.

The Faithful Couple

twine us to our fate
to bed here spring on spring

root-bound,
deepening

your life is my life
our skins coarsening,

I bear your bones,
I bear your bones on me

Wawona Tunnel Tree

slashed and burned
I screamed
needles and cones
raped me

until I healed, re-grew,
scarring to a bridge,
laced with

children's heads
gleaming and shining,
brief

chunks of me excised
bled sap, wept
as they tunneled
with their passing

my tissue
stronger than before
reparation

inside me now
so curiously
in their passing

The Vegetable Lamb

Indeed, according to the early and uncultured belief of certain communities, there are various kinds of animal-producing trees, accounts of which are very curious. Among these may be mentioned the vegetable lamb. To quote Sir John Maundeville, who in his 'Voyage and Travel' has recorded many fabulous sights:—"There grows a manner of fruit as though it were gourdes; and when they are ripe men cut them in two, and find within a little beast, dressed in flesh, bone and blood as though it were a lamb without wool—and men eat both the fruit and the beast, and that is a great marvel." Its local name is the Scythian or Tartarian Lamb; and, as it grows, it might be taken for an animal rather than a vegetable production. It is of the genus Polypodium; root decumbent, thickly clothed with a soft hoal of a deep yellow hue. A Chinese nickname is "Rufous dog." Fluid is said to flow from it when cut or injured, which originates in the fact the fresh root when slit yields a tenacious gum akin to the blood of a virgin, a crimson sap one might infer tastes delectable as honey.

Green Giant

Oh, I was a gundiguts all right,
a fat pursy fellow
but my sensibilities were fine, for a giant.

My henges were stunning. I laid
them down like dominoes, learnt to tell
the time. I was rooted to the earth,

swifts blasting past my eyelashes,
skylarks warbling stereo.
I could suck streams dry, flick gates

into spillikins, pull up hedges,
shake their treasures out.
But I didn't. I liked to watch

the wheels of weather, rolling
purple clouds like thoughts,
the lip of sun curving up, melting away.

I'd sit on the plains, on top of the world
on my fine chalk horse, stroke cows
the size of freckles, dip fingertips

in hives, stand, like an oak,
dripping honey, till moths settled
in my palms, sipping, tickling.

I named them all – little snout, cream wave,
ruddy dagger wing –
sometimes I felt like God

but even giants grow old. And lonely.
It's all so far away. So I laid my legs
over Dorset, my head on Wiltshire's pillow,

guts spilling into Somerset,
lost myself in deep slow slumber,
until you swaddled me tighter and tighter

in rags of oil seed rape. Now I can't
stop waking up, raising my sloped head,
crushing every stinking bud to pulp.

The Great Pacific Garbage Patch

All century trash floated round the gyre
of the Pacific: bright and shiny, shoes
baked themselves open, grew weedy gills,
shoals of rolling bottles nudged each other,
blister packs burst delicately –
the scent of rubber wove itself round
chair legs like a cat.

    There were swirls of wilted condoms,
ribbed and stippled, a shining dummy teat,
slowly turning tyres: the stuff of shucked
and cast-off lives, cresting rills of milky foam,
breeding in long nests of hair.

    Worst of all in the warm clutter
were the shopping bags of every shade,
plaited by the waves' regular hand
or domed, translucent as a bloom of medusae,
ripped membranes flickering like something precious.

    One day when the sky hung heavy,
I gunned the outboard motor, ducked the boom
to take a closer look. The brine was thick,
sounding a thin high note like a bell.

    Mass jostled for attention,
each piece sliding and mounting the other
as if silence pushed it out of the sea,
back into my hands, offering it up.

Sentinel

Let me tell you about life this autumn
how it's searching for its bearings, its foetal pole,
something of magnetic north, of calibrations,
growing inch by inch into the real, a quickening
towards a different future, by ancient design.
The weed under the water moves so slowly
pulled by a gibbous moon, the familiar coinage
of the female form, her land-locked body's tides.
How from the tube's frayed gape floats an egg
and how one seed might pierce its seamless skin,
set it dividing, tumbling into a stranger,
strange as the man in the moon, the women
three-mothers-back, who look like you but are not you,
whose gentle songs echo the final reckoning ...
of this she sings, my pulsar, my canary.

Lambskin

Write me a lambsong,
sing me a skin, yellow curls
coming through, curling to wool,
to warmth, long as a long tongue licking me –
filling my cells with milk.

We stole the lambskin –
I roll on its song,
we took its song, its young song,
unrolled the curves
laid them over our flat hills.

She places me at the core
where its heart grew –
I am naked in a pool of wool
floating my bones in chambers of air,
lamb wool singing me.

Outside the ewes are calling,
I am the cry and she comes.

Little Red

Were you made from an act of love?
             Perhaps, but I calculated
the best day for it, upended my rear
for you to enter the eye and when we finished
moving, we were tied like dogs –

together we smelt like the underside of fresh fish,
salt fresh fish
and I knew, then, we'd done all we could,
and when I tested you, delved, something
echoed back, faint and feint and faintly blue,
a presence like a cursor, a plus sign, a positive
you were here, more than a thought,
now a dividing self.
             I left you to grow
in my mind, seeding,
your seed-self sown, I carried you
from conception to the knowledge
that something was there, something,
a heartbeat like a pretzel
twisting in the sonic dark, twisting and pulsing,
holding on to life. And then you stopped
the manner of growing, made from the same dream
as your siblings,
and I lay in the bath and watched a star
blinking far off in the dark, I watched the star
over the road,
and I let you fall away, smallest of our being
into brilliant red; the brightest red I've known.

Pox Charm

If a man has water elf disease
his nails are dark and his eyes ooze.

Take feverfew, hassock, the stem of fane,
green lichen from the cross,
lupin, helenium, strawberry leaves
fen mint, dill, and lily
and bind them in a cloth.

Soak the herbs in holy water,
sing a litany, the Credo
and the Paternoster,
then feed him milk and purest water
and sing this out again:

I have bound the strongest bandages
So the wounds neither burn or burst
Or leap or spread or deepen.
May he keep in a healthy way,
And ache no more than it aches Earth.

Write Christ's mark on each limb.
All will soon be well with him.

Charm for Delayed Birth

Let the woman who cannot carry her bairn
go to the grave, step three times over
say, *earth, earth, mother of earth,*
help me against late birth, the lame –

and when that woman goes to rest
with her beloved man in bed
may he feed and tend to her,
say, *up you go, over you step,*

full with our first-born birthling,
swelling and fattening, ripening,
and when the mother senses
the quickening and the dropping,

woman with a cradle she cannot fill,
let her go to a child's resting place
pick a flower from the grave,
wrap it in black wool and throw the petals

far, like bad corn, far away,
then let her draw milk from the mildest
beast and sip it from her palm,
take her to the stream to say,

everywhere I have carried you
strong, tight and firm
and I shall carry you until you are born
and then I shall carry you home.

Charm for a Lost Child

Sister: I bring you woundwort –
we'll pack your heart and staunch the flow,
cut a wand of yew
against love returned cold.

Soon you will stop bleeding –
we'll leave him on a trestle,
scattered with feverfew, sew sprigs
for a shroud to keep him so.

Sister: you shall strengthen
as the moon fattens,
your blood ripening –
I'll take you to the nettles

their fierce bite, the boys cut down,
our mother bending willow
and we'll dress him in butterbur, dear sister,
fairest yarrow.

Little rough one of the moors,
take these beneath your pillow:
nine stalks of royal fern,
foxglove flowers, fennel,

three bones of an old man
newly torn from the charnel.
We'll burn these on embers,
smear the dust over our breasts

and sister, against the cold stone,
the sea's hand, the wormy rose
he shall not wither away
but grow as true love grows.

Hare

Throw her head into fire,
hare becomes dawn,
racing her creep over the shadow.

Moon slits hare's lip,
slits with her silver finger nail,
silver crescent rocking.

Or, hare laughs so,
she splits her lip:
no seamstress here.

Hare is pregnant,
corn spirit, lying low,
when caught she cries like a child.

What ankle spokes, what spine.
Hare unboned, in flux
jester-eared, shouldering air.

Moon draws a fingernail
over the rising land
showing hare the way.

Over she goes in the moonlight
over and over like a fantasy.

Mass

When she left, the bees arrived
upon the sandstone church,
they balled as a growth that seeded wild,
hung, heavy as a breast.

Onto the sacred wall they gathered
dripping low hymns,
each body tremulous, lit with sound,
one emphatic lung.

Bound by a net of pheromone
they came to her and they clung,
not to sting yet thick with intent,
something urging them on

and as we left the church in file,
they were black against the sun
lifting and scattering to bless
the body of their queen.

Messenger

We found her in the shadow
of the gas drum;
a pleat of otherness
pinched from her dominion.

Maw like a whale,
head slit to gill air,
a dark scythe
at our feet.

We willed her wings to open
her form take shape,
conflate to airy spaces.
A new crescent moon.

We picked the whole contraption up,
brindled, tawny, creamy throat;
she spilled over our hands
into awe.

Her claws were shriven,
her eyes the eyes
of something fallen,
the weight unbearable

so we sent her onwards,
to beat at the heels
of a young god's sandals,
set her away, windward.

May

Then may I be Queen again
stepping through the cow parsley,
dog behind my shadow-train,
children waiting, patiently,
and all the fruit in the land
to ripen, all the bees working,
life in my hands, warm and pliant,
the music of my heart
defiant and now
                    the umbels hang
their heads, push stars
of whiteness every May;
they grow on over me, the dog,
our rustling passageway,
close behind us, bright heads bowing.

Still Life

Start with an open prospect:
choose your site carefully.
A little poverty is necessary –
use natural materials, though,
no plastic sacking or corrugated iron
but hollow trunks, tumble-down briars,
a weathered stile.
Now bring in various accidents
of weather – loosen stones,
tumble them into irregular masses.
Add Sedum, Sweet William,
pad out your scene with props:
consult field guides for the correct
species. Remember cows
look best in groups of three.
Be true to your season –
a weave of gnats, or a bank of
cumuli add an extra layer of fact.
Try to make it work close up –
distress cob walls,
give gates moss, a little rust to hint
at passing time. Don't forget
the crowning point – draw the eye
with an evening star, a wedge
of geese – I've chosen this
cascade of ivy, gilded each leaf
with long strokes of light.

Sculpting a Mole

How can I let you free, dandy quarry,
your snout a star;

in my hands
you are slack, irresistible, mandibled,
lowly, costly rarity –

noonshirker, beastly sock,
wriggler, digger,
didgery-do-not-touch

part shoveller, part saviour,
aerator, blind architect,
worrier –

warm in my palm,
you are gone,
sleuthed clean of your bindings –

The Cannots

They are afraid of dolls.
Their genitals are dry.

They are drawn to mountains and motorways.
There have no fear of flying.

Their temper cannot be lost – it is chained
like a dear dog.

They think the Bible is valiant.
They love the way starfish can grow back a limb.

They cannot come, or hiccup,
but convincingly fake both.

They can see through our clothes, into our guts,
read what we are made of.

They are always on the surface of the sea –
they cannot get wet.

They cannot drown either: they loiter
on the inter-tidal zone.

They use onions or pepper to cry
when watching soap operas or weddings.

Their feet are always very pretty,
soles soft as a new-born.

They learn white lies, learn to tell them like a joke.
If they win a race it is not deliberate.

They make vigilant life-guards and paramedics.
They like to think about magic.

Music does not work
but their singing voices are always astounding.

They remember every birth,
find the vanishing point in shop windows,

walk over hot coals, and pray
one day, they might burn.

The Green Flash

At the precise moment of his departure,
my father came to me in the cockpit, heading west.
We were flying to the gold coast and the sun disc was sinking,
we were primed to the horizon as we are trained to be,
great banks of cumuli pink beneath the fuselage,
we were primed to the tangents and quadrants of atmosphere,
following the earth's curvature, 269 souls on board,
and a box of birds in the cargo hold,
when I felt a pain in my heart, right under my pilot's wings,
it was sharp and sudden like treading on a pin, deep
into your heel flesh, and the green ray shot up,
a blaze from the upper rim, like a peak in a cardiograph,
and I blinked and the pain blinked and the green spiked itself
over the falling sun, over the unobstructed horizon,
it flared and flew for one, maybe two seconds, green to blue
to violet as a bruise.

And Then He Started Singing Again

And then he started singing again
and a bucket load of beer-vomit came whooshing out
I'm too drunk to feel the pain if you hit me, and if you kill me
I'll be glad to be dead
and then he started singing again
When you, my darling, are gone
howling away at the filthy songs of his fathers
not in a stinking world like this
what sort of a world is it? men on the moon and men
spinning round the earth like it might be midges round a lamp
and then it was blood, not song nor vomit
that came out of his filthy mouth
and brought thee peace and victory
then we tripped him so he laid down flat and heavy
but still he went on singing
he was sort of flattened to the wall and his platties
were a disgrace that was disgusting
so we gave him the boot, one go each
he shut up singing and started to creech
oh dear dear land, I fought for thee
then he gave us some lip music
go on, do me in you bastard cowards,
I don't want to live anyway
and I will go back to my darling, my darling
so we got hold of him and cracked him,
but he still went on singing
so we cracked into him lovely, grinning all over our faces
it's no world for any old man any longer
and then he started singing again

Charm Against a Wen

Wen, wen, little wen
You are not welcome here –
Go north to the far, hard hills
Where your wretched brother waits.

He shall lay a leaf over your face
Roll you under the wolf's heavy paw,
Feed you to the eagle's talon
And you shall writhe and shrivel.

Fade, like coal on the hearth.
Shrink and flake like dung in the light.
Waste as water in the pail,
small as a grain of linseed,
            tinier than a hand-worm's hipbone!

So tiny you are   nothing
            wen, wen, wen.

Black and Blue

Black is the colour of my true love's hair
and sea blue are his eyes
but brown is where my duty lies
and brown is my despair.

I rise at dawn and tend to him
my brown-eyed concubine
but black is the colour of my true love's hair
and blacker still my mind.

I look into my husband's eyes
and swim within the brown
but black is the colour of my true love's hair
and sea blue are his eyes –

black as the sky on midnight's chime
and blue as brilliant day
black and blue are my sweetheart's lies
but brown is what I bear.

Cannibal

Once I was so hungry, I tore the skin in strips from my feet
and ate it – a masseuse asked *if I was burned?*
There was protein there. I ate stories too,
tales of survival in the shell of planes.

People are said to taste like pork,
the Polynesians called white folk *long pigs* –
Did you know we'd all taste ourselves
all day long, if we could; that's what poems are for.

I'd never eat a child.
I'd sooner die than eat a sibling.
Pork meat is white, fatty, fibrous
with the same strings that animate human days.

I'd like to think I could stay alive
on rain and my own dermis, beads of breast milk,
crusts of wax. My heart quietly consuming itself,
cardiac walls breaking down.

Eyas

I tread her wrist and wear the hood,
talons sunk into the seize,
cry of myself, and I draw blood –

the curving air, the streaming world
rise in the rings of my dark eyes,
I tread her wrist and wear the hood.

Locked in my mews, the world in bud,
I raise my wings, push to rouse,
cry to myself, and I taste blood –

my scalloped robes are wet with blood,
the lure is close, the creance pulls,
I tread her wrist and wear the hood.

I keen to bank above the wood
my shadow like a falling cross,
I cry of this, and taste the blood,

its beat within my jewelled hood,
bewits dragging down the skies.
I tread her wrist and wear the hood,
I cry of this, and I draw blood.

Oxygen

We took it in together:

planes banking on tiers of sky,
and underneath two cabbage whites
tying knots in the air,
petals on the closing daisy,
lashes round the ox's eye.
Later the pipistrelle,
its loopy figure of eight,
later still the moth,
its ragged orbit still its own
around its own hot sun.
And binding this our blood,
its start and finish, its brilliance,
the give-and-take
and give of oxygen.

Owls

I carry the owls with me
deep in my pocket or tucked
in the cup of my bra: they doze,
bills dipped in a bib of feathers,
turn janglesome if I forget they
are there when I run for the bus.
They come with me to work:
warm-blooded and tickly as fingers.
We sit in the road, the owls and I,
lost in the dwining day, the failing
sun a shinicle over the town.
I carry their flight over dreaming
hills, hollow bones lifting
and keening. They gowl for slumgullion,
cagmag, fresh mice: get shifty
as we reach the back country,
tear through my blouse,
glide over the spinney, searching,
searching –

I carry the owls with me, still,
in vellum and in sepia. I carry
them on my tongue and I feed them
to our children. May they carry the owls
for us all, their darknesses, their eyes.

We Are Listening

through the bars
of our blinds at tea-time –
through orange nights
cupped ears tilt
towards the stars.

We hear, sometimes,
the tines of space,
thin and insistent,
constant as light, as
our knowledge of the moon.

There are whispers in
horoscopes
as Mercury regresses;
we hear spring tides –
their reach beyond the shore.

We are listening
in stadia, rising as one,
in choirs and in the sofa department
of out-of-town stores
as light pools onto the Saturday boy.

There are conversations, sometimes,
in back catalogues,
in the grain of very old tables;
a dialogue between barcodes
and desire –

we are listening for an answer
to our selves; why
stars in the vastness sing,
and nothing answers,
answers nothing at all.

Afterlife

The marshes have filled themselves
with wetness and bird song
since they were left alone.
The Basran reed warbler breeds
deep in Mesopotamian banks,
the original garden of Eden.

Each dusk, birds with dark eyestripes
flash amber shadows low
over lakes and gleaming mud.
So many species are flourishing,
the African darter, the sacred ibis –
one day women in libraries, flocks of singing girls.

Cloud

this cloud is not a real cloud
it cannot rain, it can rain
no longer/this is a server
with cabled snakes.

this cloud is around us,
do angels live there?
we over-write our shadows,
we over-write our lines.

i weigh nothing in this photo,
you weigh nothing in this photo.
this cloud bears so much
heat it burns.

Notes and Acknowledgments

Downy Mildew
Dr Dillon Weston made models of *Bremia lactucae* (downy mildew) using glass rods and a Bunsen burner.

The Vegetable Lamb
Adapted from a passage taken from *The Folk-lore of Plants* by T. F. Thiselton-Dyer, 1889.

Pox Charm
Translated from the Anglo Saxon Metrical Charm 7: For the Water-Elf Disease. Thought to be chicken pox.

With acknowledgment to Karen Louise Jolly, author of *Popular Religion in Late Saxon England: Elf Charms in Context* (University of North Carolina Press, 1996).

Charm for a Lost Child
Inspired by a love charm in *Carmina Gadelica: Hymns and Incantations*, collected by Alexander Carmichael, 1900.

And Then He Started Singing Again
Poem composed using the random integer generator with lines taken from *A Clockwork Orange* by Anthony Burgess, pp. 14–15.

Black and Blue
'Black is the colour of my true love's hair' is the title of a traditional folk song, thought to have originated from Scotland, later re-worked by Nina Simone.

Eyas
Inspired by a line from Robert Duncan's poem 'My Mother Would Be a Falconress'.

Cloud
The Cermak data centre, in Illinois, forms the 'backbone' of the internet with thousands of computer servers and hundreds of miles of cables providing cloud storage.

Thanks are due to the editors of the following publications where some of these poems first appeared: *Artemis, Best British Poetry 2014* (Salt), *Butcher's Dog, Days of Roses, The Guardian Online, The Interpreter's House, Horizon Review, Magma, Mslexia, The Poetry Review, Poetry Wales, Lung Jazz: Young British Poets for Oxfam* (Cinnamon), *Where Rockets Burn Through: Contemporary Science Fiction Poems* (Penned in the Margins), *Snap* (Templar), *Ware Poets Anthology*.

Some of these poems were previously published in a pamphlet, *Inklings* (Flipped Eye, 2013), which was a winner in The Venture Award.

'Downy Mildew' was first published in *Pocket Horizon* (Valley Press, 2013) as part of a collaboration with The Whipple Museum, Cambridge, and The Wellcome Collection in London.

Some of the charm poems were written during the 'Voiced' writers' residency at Bethnal Green Nature Reserve, London, 2015.

I would especially like to thank the following for support, insight and inspiration: The Nevada Street Poets, Deryn Rees-Jones, Wilson Weaver and all at Liverpool University Press, Myra Schneider, Kathryn Maris, and my family near and far.